THE
Archive Photographs
SERIES

FIVE

STROUD

PHOTOGRAPHERS

JOHN AND MATILDA MERRETT, UMBRELLA MAKERS OF STROUD, c. 1882. In one of the earliest Merrett Bros. photographs, Mark Merrett's parents, John and Matilda, sit fashionably attired, proudly displaying examples of their trade. Despite his patriarchal appearance, John was only in his mid fifties when this photograph was taken.

Previous page: STROUD SHOW, 1913. In this photograph by George and Adèle Stone, the procession passes down Rowcroft on its way to Fromehall Park.

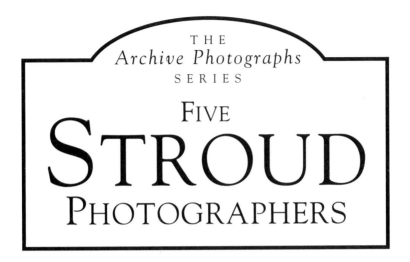

THE
Archive Photographs
SERIES

FIVE

STROUD

PHOTOGRAPHERS

Compiled by
Howard Beard, Peter Harris and Wilfred Merrett

CHALFORD

The Chalford Publishing Company
St Mary's Mill, Chalford,
Stroud, Gloucestershire, GL6 8NX

ISBN 0 7524 0305 2

Typesetting and origination by
The Chalford Publishing Company
Printed in Great Britain by
Redwood Books, Trowbridge

LUNCH ALFRESCO, c. 1910. Mark Merrett, on the right, joins his future wife's family for Sunday lunch at their home in Eastington. The older generation appear very warmly clad for what is, presumably, a summer's day.

W.F. LEE. This photograph was taken in the 1920s after Lee had moved to Cheltenham. The pride he felt in owning a motor vehicle is self-evident.

Contents

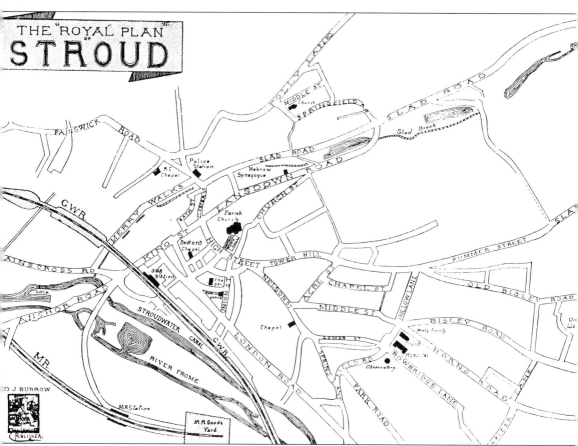

MAP OF STROUD. Burrows of Cheltenham produced this plan for their 1902 District Guide.

Acknowledgements

The authors would like to thank: G. Adams, B. Aldridge, P. Aston, D. Burton, Mrs A. Cook, D. Cope, A. Davis, S. Gardiner, B. Ginger, Mrs T. Harris, Mrs V. Harvey, Mrs N. Holmes, R. Jordan, Mrs I. MacKellaig, Mrs B. Merrett, the late W. Mills, B. Moss, the late L. Padin, R. Perrett, Miss P. Pinnell, J. Sollars, Mrs P. Tuck, Mrs J. Tucker, P. Walmsley, L. Walrond, W.O. Wicks and the readers of the *Stroud News and Journal* for their help in identifying photographs. The authors are especially grateful to Sylvia Beard for typing the text.

PUNCH AND JUDY SHOW. This detail is taken from a photograph of street entertainment at The Cross in Stroud and is one of W.F. Lee's finest pictures.

Introduction

At no time in Britain's history has the appearance and character of our towns and landscapes altered more rapidly than in the present century. It is perhaps unsurprising, therefore, that the work of those photographers who recorded the social scene in Edwardian England should hold an especial fascination today, as both the century and the millenium draw to a close.

By 1900, photography was, of course, becoming a less complex affair than it had been in the 1860s. Technical improvements both in cameras and in developing allowed professional and skilled amateur photographers alike the freedom to capture on film, with increasing ease, the changing scene. Better transport for the photographer coincided in 1902 with new Post Office regulations permitting the whole area of one side of a postcard to be given over to a pictorial image. All these factors in combination led to an almost feverish obsession for collecting picture postcards: henceforth, no corner of rural or industrial Britain was safe from the photographer's prying lens.

In spite of these improvements, some established photographers continued to work solely within the familiar confines of their studios. But soon every city and town – and many larger villages too – boasted a postcard photographer exploring the pictorial potential of his home patch. Stroud was no exception. During the period before the First World War, the town and its surroundings were photographed extensively not only by such local photographers as Mark

COMLEY'S PHOTOGRAPH OF A SPLENDIDLY COSTUMED GROUP FROM THE HISTORICAL PAGEANT OF 1911.

Merrett, W.F. Lee, the Stones and Henry Comley, but also by national firms such as Francis Frith, Valentine and Hartmann.

Mark Merrett, father of co-author Wilfred, established his business well back in the nineteenth century, principally as a studio portrait firm: for him, expansion into serious topographical work was a natural progression, a sensitive response to public demand. When, around 1902, Henry Comley took over J.H. Elliott's equally long-founded business, he followed the same path.

In the period after 1900, W.F. Lee and the Stones both represent newly established concerns. William Adams has been included here as an example of a photographer of a new generation. In the 1920s and 1930s Adams, whose work is almost exclusively topographical rather than portrait-based, recorded landscapes and townscapes very considerably different from those his Edwardian predecessors saw. The contrast is fascinating.

In this book, where appropriate, items of ephemera have been used to highlight the subject matter of the pictures. Similarly, events or places covered by more than one photographer (for example, the Dudbridge blackbird or the 1907 Agricultural Show) have been cross-referenced.

The photographers chosen for this study need not have numbered a mere five: throughout the first forty years of this century there were many other private individuals and notable professionals whose work was of a high quality and might usefully be brought together in print on another occasion. The five we have selected do, however, offer an excellent insight into the physical and social development of Stroud and its immediate environs in the years up to the beginning of the Second World War. The importance of their work lies in the record it provides of missing buildings, lost landscapes and vanished examples of street furniture; perhaps it also touches that nostalgic chord which most of us have, yet prefer to suppress.

One

Mark Merrett

The seventh of the thirteen children of John Merrett, the local umbrella maker, Mark was born at 4, Tower Hill, near to The Cross in Stroud. His formal education began at the Blackboy School at the tender age of two years and eight months and ceased eight years later. Voluntary attendance at night school followed.

Mark had very varied occupations during his teenage years and, showing some artistic ability, secured an apprenticeship with Mr Hughes, a photographer in Swan Lane. Initially training as a retoucher, Mark proved a quick learner and soon mastered the rudiments of photography.

MARK MERRETT. This portrait of Mark was taken at the firm's Russell Street Studio c.1900.

At the age of twenty-two, he felt sufficiently confident to branch out on his own and, joined by his younger brother George, acquired basic equipment and rented premises in Jamaica Road, Bermondsey. This London enterprise proved a success but, due to family problems in Stroud, the brothers returned home and, a year later, established their business in a wooden studio erected in the Corn Exchange yard. After a year or two this building was re-erected on a site at the top of Russell Street, where it remained for some sixty years, latterly occupied by the Art Memorial Company. The firm, known as Merrett Bros., operated from the Russell Street premises for some forty years, although George left the partnership during the 1890s. The business prospered and Mark employed several assistants, including a young lady retoucher who later became his wife. A devout member of the Plymouth Brethren, Mark's high principles influenced his whole life and he believed in producing good quality work at affordable prices.

Prior to the First World War, Mark was joined by his younger brother Rayner, who had been apprenticed to the trade in Weston-super-Mare before running a business in Barton Street, Gloucester. Additional premises had already been rented at 7 George Street and Rayner obtained the services of Gertrude Peacey, a retoucher who had formerly worked for Stone and Comley.

Although primarily portrait photographers, Merrett Bros. had published postcard views from the turn of the century, and these included not only nearby beauty spots but also local events, architectural commissions, school groups, disasters and advertising. Public transport was used to convey the cumbersome equipment to scenic locations, although both partners used motor cars for a short period in the 1920s.

Following Mark's retirement in 1923 he continued to operate in a part-time capacity from a studio erected behind his house in Belle Vue Road. During the next twenty years he had a limited number of 'sitters', but much preferred to take local postcard views, which were sold for a few pence in village shops and post offices. Rayner, meanwhile, had moved to premises in Lansdown where, following his premature death in 1929, his widow continued the business for a further thirty or more years.

The Merrett photographic connection with Stroud had thus lasted for over eighty years.

THE CORN EXCHANGE. Merrett Bros.' first local studio was erected in the Corn Exchange yard at the top of the High Street c. 1884 and a display case showing examples of their work was hung from the railings. It was not an ideal situation and, after a year or so, the studio was removed to a better site in Russell Street.

Opposite: PHOTOGRAPH BACKS. The backs of Victorian and Edwardian photographs were frequently embellished with elaborate art work; these Merrett examples are no exception. The reference number shown on the Russell Street photograph back gives some indication of the volume of work carried out by the firm.

Merrett Bros.

TOP OF RUSSELL ST.
ADJOINING LONDON RD.
STROUD.

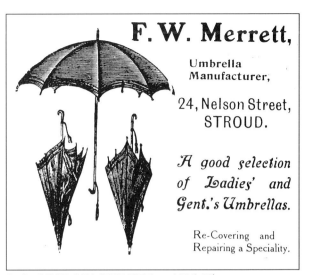

Left: GEORGE MERRETT, c. 1895. This portrait of George, with his son Christopher, dates from shortly before he left the partnership to resume his trade as umbrella maker in Bath.

Above: UMBRELLA ADVERTISEMENT. Mark's younger brother, Frederick, continued the family umbrella-making trade in Stroud until his death in 1919. The business was first established in Wiltshire by his grandfather in 1828 and remained in the family until 1930.

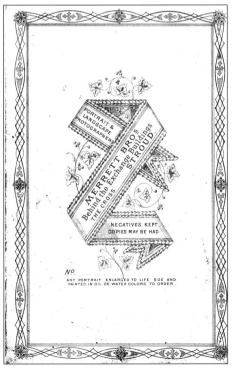

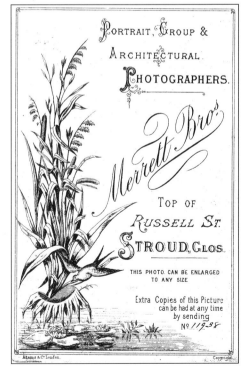

STUDIO INTERIOR, 1904. This was most probably the George Street Studio, as it closely resembles the photograph which appeared in the 1902 *Stroud Illustrated Guide* of the interior of the premises Merrett took over from Joseph Smith, another local photographer. Miss Elizabeth Gay is seated in the centre, with Miss Jeanette Cratchley on the right. Note the elaborate roller-mounted backdrop, portrait camera and profusion of chairs, pedestals, stools etc., all part of a photographer's stock-in-trade.

Opposite: TRADE EXHIBITION, 1907. The Stroud Subscription Rooms provided the venue for this exhibition, with the Merrett Bros.' stand 'manned' by the Misses Gay and Cratchley. A large range of local postcards is displayed on a rotating rack and a notice states 'Enlargements finished in any style.' Miss Gay sits behind a table laden with sundry photographic accessories, including a stereoscope.

RUSSELL STREET, 1905. The Merrett Bros.' studio, liberally stocked with postcards and examples of portraiture, is on the extreme left, next to the premises occupied by W. Wells and Son, jewellers. Mr Sidney Pearce, the saddler, is seen emerging from the adjoining shop.

WALTER MERRETT'S UMBRELLA SHOP. During the early 1920s, Mark helped his elder brother Walter (pictured with wife Rosa) to set up in business in Ebley. Half of the window space was allocated to Walter's utilitarian display, the remainder being occupied by examples of Merrett Bros.' work. Unfortunately, the venture was short-lived, on account of Walter's ill health. The youngsters standing outside the shop would be octogenarians if alive today!

BELLE VUE ROAD, c. 1925. The two semi-detached houses on the left were occupied by Rayner and Mark Merrett respectively, Mark's garden providing space for a large studio. Both properties were demolished for roadwidening in the early 1970s. Part of Tower House, which gave its name to Tower Hill (now Parliament Street), can be seen on the right. Note the unmetalled road surface.

VIEW FROM BELLE VUE ROAD, c. 1930. Sixty years ago this road was a pleasant residential backwater. The attractive buildings bordering the road have since been demolished, apart from the cottage on the extreme right with its neat garden, which looks much the same today. The old vicarage, St Roses' Convent and the School of Art are clearly visible.

CHURCH STREET, c. 1920. A rather atmospheric view showing the old almshouses and adjacent properties that were demolished over forty years ago to create a carpark. Note how the inclusion of the baker's boy and background loiterers brings the scene to life.

CHURCH STREET, c. 1930. A later view taken by Mark Merrett, following his removal to the Belle Vue Road Studio. The Parish Church and Vicarage (now a nursing home) remain, the rest of the buildings having been destroyed in the name of progress! With regard to the Vicarage, a former incumbent considered he had been provided with 'a champagne house on a beer income!' Apart from the sweet and tobacconist's shop shown on the right, a cobbler, a plumber and, later, a veterinary surgeon had premises in this street. During World War Two it was also the location of a house of ill repute!

BRICKROW, c. 1920. The 'new buildings' referred to formed a large extension to Holloway's Clothing Factory which, at one time, employed over a thousand workers. The part of the building near the camera was destroyed by fire in 1992, a similar fate having befallen the gabled premises on the left, occupied by Bown's Mineral Water business, many years earlier. The name Brickrow derives from a long rank of brick cottages, most of which were demolished early this century to make room for the factory.

THE CROSS. Relatively few photographs exist of upper Stroud and this superb view probably dates from c. 1920. The drinking fountain, embellished with dolphins, stood in front of buildings removed in 1930 to make way for the Stroud Co-operative Society's new department store. Bradshaw's busy greengrocery premises are prominent on the right, beyond the Crown Inn. Both buildings were removed to make way for the Cornhill Relief Road. The handcart belonged to Mr Philpotts, a cobbler who, as a sideline, transported packages to and from the town's railway station.

CASTLE STREET. A girl sits beside an upturned bench in front of the well-known Blackboy School. This building, erected in 1844, served as a girls' elementary school for many years, prior to becoming a teachers' centre. The large notice board on the left draws attention to the morning and evening services at the adjacent Wesleyan Chapel, since converted into flats. The board on the railings on the right reads 'Roxburgh House Red Cross Hospital', possibly its use during the Boer War, as this photograph dates from very early in the century.

BAZAAR

IN AID OF BUILDING A

New Wesleyan Chapel and Schools

AT STROUD.

Stroud, *3 June* 187.2

Dear *Madam*

   The Trustees for the above having decided to begin building without further delay, the Ladies of the Stroud Society and Congregation have arranged to hold a Bazaar in the Autumn, in aid of the same.

   Desirous of making it a thorough success, they now earnestly appeal to their friends for contributions, either in money, or goods of any saleable description.

WESLEYAN BAZAAR, 1872. This rather tattered but interesting fund-raising leaflet has somehow survived from the period just prior to the building of Castle Street Chapel in the 1870s.

LOCKING HILL. A solitary schoolboy poses for the camera in this view, taken c. 1910, looking towards Slad Road. Immediately in front of the house in the centre stands an elaborate aviary or gazebo. All the houses on the extreme left were demolished to make way for a ring-road which never materialized. The site is now occupied by a doctors' surgery.

OVER COURT NURSING HOME. During the 1930s this large house in Slad Road was used as a private nursing home. 'Sister' Kate Treharne was in charge, assisted by Nurse Lewes-Jones, amongst others. Miss Treharne, a devout Christian lady, is standing nearest the camera, with Miss Lewes-Jones on the left. The writer recalls the overpowering scent of geraniums in the front porch.

JOHN STREET BAPTIST CHURCH. This building dates from 1824, the later addition of porch and vestibule being removed in 1976. Holloway's original factory, later converted into offices for the Stroud Rural District Council, adjoins the church. John and Matilda Merrett, the photographer's parents, were married here in 1847.

JOHN STREET BAPTIST CHURCH INTERIOR. This photograph shows to advantage the impressive organ, and the elaborate ironwork, which dates from 1879, enclosing the pulpit area and gallery.

ST ALBAN'S CHURCH INTERIOR. This simple Byzantine-Romanesque building was converted from part of Stroud's original workhouse as a memorial to the much-loved Father Stanton, an Anglo-Catholic priest born at Upfield, Paganhill. The church is now jointly used by Anglicans and Methodists.

UPLANDS 'TIN' CHURCH, c. 1908. This structure, at the lower end of Middle Street, served the spiritual needs of Uplands until replaced by the new All Saints' Church in 1910 (see page 61). Stonehouse P.C.C. acquired and removed the building for use as a church hall. It later became a cinema, until destroyed by fire in 1936. A similar building can still be seen at Thrupp.

FOLLY LANE. On a fine summer's day, Mr. Gardiner wends his way towards Stroud, having just passed the pretty cottage on the right. Note the tiny bridges spanning the ditch separating cottage from road. A tinted postcard, showing the same scene, was given free to customers of Stroud's former large drapery and furniture store, Messrs Lewis and Godfrey.

FOLLY LANE. The same view in winter. Mr. Gardiner, undeterred, carefully picks his way though the snow. The cottage looks snug. Its tall chimney was needed to create a better draught. Sadly, progress has taken its toll: the road has been widened and the cottage replaced by a massive reconstructed stone wall. It is recalled that a farm wagon once ran into the ditch, tipping its load of hay over the cottage, which virtually disappeared.

STROUD FROM FOLLY LANE. Uplands School and a few farm buildings marked Stroud's extremities in 1930: no sign yet of the large housing developments that would cover much of the rural foreground in years to come. 'The Folly,' was an isolated cottage further up the lane, since replaced by a modern residence.

UPPER STROUD, c. 1930. The Victorian expansion of Stroud between Holy Trinity Church and the workhouse is clearly visible in this photograph. Park Road provides access to the large residences of the Field Estate, built in the 1880s, but the paddocks adjoining London Road remain undeveloped. Eagle Mill and the Bowbridge Dyeworks can be seen lower right.

STROUD VALLEY MOTOR, c. 1905. For some years this steam-powered carriage operated between Chalford and Stonehouse and, later, Gloucester. The photograph comprehensively includes the Thames and Severn Canal, Arundel Mill Dyeworks, with its forest of chimneys, and the old Midland Railway stables, extreme left. (Another railcar photograph is on page 102.)

HORNS FARM. Although only a mile from the centre of Stroud, the pleasant Horns valley is little changed and remains popular with both walker and rider. Note the stepped boundary wall of the old cemetery and the former Target Inn, top right.

PAGANHILL, 1920. There have been no great changes here, although the cottage partly visible in the centre has gone. Perhaps the photographer invited the children on the extreme right to pose for the picture, but they preferred to remain modestly in the wings. The message reads, 'This is a real photo of Paganhill; you know the place quite well; Mrs White's the shop and Mrs Haynes' white gate. You can just see our door where a little girl is standing and Mr Clark the tailor's shop, and on the left you can see Randwick and at the very top the Rising Sun.' The recipient of the postcard was the wife of a prison officer at Parkhurst. (There are further pictures of Paganhill on pages 120 and 121.)

FARMHILL, STROUD. Few could identify this rural scene today. The pond, fed by the Ruscombe stream, has been infilled; the land to the right is occupied by Archway School and building development: houses and bungalows have replaced the old Farmhill Park glasshouses on the skyline. The card is postmarked 1924 and the writer had just cycled from Stroud to Camp and Painswick.

CAINSCROSS SUNDIAL. This elaborate milestone stood for many years in the garden of the Sundial Café at the top of Bridge Street. Now lacking its gnomons and capped with protective stonework, it stands in isolation outside Tricorn House.

NETHER LYPIATT MANOR. Known locally as ' The Haunted House', this fine building was erected by Judge Coxe c. 1710. Legend has it that a blacksmith, under sentence of death, was reprieved to enable him to make the elaborate entrance gates, but when the Judge discovered a minor irregularity in the ironwork, the unfortunate fellow was executed. A small obelisk in the grounds commemorates a later owner's favourite horse, 'Wag'. As dormer windows were inserted in the roof in 1923, the photograph must have been taken some time earlier.

SHADY NOOK AT WEYHOUSE. The tiny cottage community at Weyhouse has long disappeared; only a few scattered stones and mullions remain. This attractive spot is close by, but it might be difficult to identify it precisely today.

HAYMAKING SCENE. The location of this lovely rural scene is not known, but it cannot be far from Stroud. The photograph was taken during the time of the Great War, which may be why the farm workers appear to be over military age. Work has temporarily halted whilst farmer, wife and young son pose with the haymakers.

ZION CHAPEL, BUTTEROW, c. 1920. This simple but attractive former Primitive Methodist Chapel was erected in 1856 and is still used as a place of worship. A solitary gravestone commemorates Nathaniel Sutton, who died in 1888 aged 90, and his wife Jane, who died in 1882 aged 84, trustees and stalwarts of the Methodist cause.

STROUD SALVATION ARMY BAND, 1906. The band comprises a rather motley bunch, with only seven of the bandsmen wearing uniform. The sole member so far identified is Joe Hawkins, second left in the back row. It is understood that he sometimes deserted the Army to arrange his own meetings!

28

HORSE AND GROOM INN, STROUD. This well-known hostelry, in The Leazes, is the setting for a family party, probably held during the time of the Great War. Back row: Mrs Carter, Mrs Neale, Bill Beckenham, Mrs Beckenham, Mrs Mills, -?-, Mrs Aldridge, Mrs Fifield (wife of well-known local boxer Abner Fifield). Front row: Mrs MacDonald, with son in kilt, Lil Fifield, Fanny Stafford (owner of junk and second-hand clothes shop in Acre Street or Tower Hill) and Granny Partridge, in whose honour the party was held. Granny Partridge, the mother of Mrs Mills, lived to be over 100.

WORKMAN'S SAWMILLS, WOODCHESTER. During the 1914-18 war, women workers were recruited to replace men in many walks of life. This photograph shows a group of women at Workman's Sawmills together with their foreman, Henry Brinkworth, and a few teenage lads. Florrie King, the lady standing next to Mr Brinkworth, later married his son.

CASTLE STREET INFANTS' SCHOOL, c. 1931. The Headmistress, Miss Audrey Dearlove, spent many years in Stroud before retiring to London, where she died in 1987 aged 100. Back row: Reg Jefferies, Sidney Willey, -?-, ? Bennett, Ken Morgan, Lena Parker. Third row: John Critchley, Bill Warner, Clement Keene, Muriel Mills, Glenys Bennett, Wilfred Merrett, Joyce Burford, Edna Gibbs. Second row: Miss Dearlove, Dick Powell, Peggy Belton, Norman Wyman, Dennis Merrett, Maurice Duberley, Ella Cratchley, Edna Beckenham, Hazel Gabb. Front row: -?-, Bill Arkell, -?-, Bill Smith, Ruth Lewis, Norman Clark, ? Jenkins, Joyce Bayliss, ? Gabb, Fred Oldmeadow.

CHURCH STREET BOYS' SCHOOL, FORM 1B, FEBRUARY 1932. Headmaster Mr Horace Doxsey remained at the school for some forty years. Back row: Mr Doxsey, -?-, ? Cole, Ernest Mills, Wilfred Merrett, ? Owen, Desmond Pratt, -?-, Ken Warner, Bill Warner, Bill Smith, Ken Morgan, Mr R. Mullins (Asst master). Middle row: Maurice Duberley, Norman Clark, -?-, -?-, ? Phelps, 'Puffy' Wathern, Trevor Furley, Ron Smith, Bertie King. Front row: Sidney Willey, Clement Keene, Doug Feltham, ? West, -?-, Dick Powell, Bill Arkell, Tony Ball, Adam Stevens, Dennis Betterton.

BOY WITH COW. The little lad looks slightly apprehensive as he grips the rope securing the farmer's prize beast. This photograph was taken somewhere near Stroud prior to 1920.

THE HORSELESS CARRIAGE. Mr W. Bolland, proprietor of the *Pike House Garage*, Avening, poses proudly at the wheel of his 1898 Darracq. The vehicle appears well-equipped, with three large headlamps, bulbous horn and vital starting handle.

THE SLAD. This attractive view of the village is enhanced by the inclusion of the two little lads and a man wending his way up the village street. The year is 1920 and the children, if not actually members of his family, are certainly contemporaries of the poet and author Laurie Lee. The message on this card reads, 'How great and how gloriously wonderful are the marvels of nature and the works of nature's omnipotence. We are invested on all sides by the marvellous panorama of the Cotswolds.' The writer's sentiments are expressed rather more succinctly by one of Mark Merrett's favourite verses of Scripture, Psalm 19, verse 1: 'The Heavens declare the glory of God and the firmament showeth his handiwork.'

THE KING STREET ARCH. This elaborate structure spanning King Street between the Royal George Hotel and Coley's chemist's shop, was one of a number erected by Philip Ford and Son at strategic positions in the town. The event in question was the 1912 Agricultural Show. Stroud had previously hosted the show, which was held each year in different towns around the county, in 1907, when a similar decorative extravaganza was provided. (See pages 50, 58-60 and 106-7.)

AMBERLEY FOUNTAIN. The village commemorated Queen Victoria's Diamond Jubilee
with this fine drinking fountain, surmounted by an ornate gas lamp which has long since
disappeared.

Two
George & Adèle Stone

George and Adèle Stone ran a husband and wife photography business at 56 London Road, Stroud, for about forty years, until George's death from a stroke in 1942. Born Ada Ellen Barnes on 28 November 1866, Adèle was the eldest daughter, in a family of eleven, of a highly proficient and much respected photographer in Ashford, Kent. George Stone, born 24 April 1864, joined the Barnes' business as an assistant and ended up marrying the boss's daughter.

GEORGE AND ADELE STONE. An informal portrait of the couple in their later years.

Before settling in Stroud, George and Adèle worked as photographers in Devizes, Leamington Spa and Swindon.

Their grand-daughter recalls that the shop window in London Road was always full of framed photographs. Behind lay the reception room, which was very often warmed by a most inviting roaring fire during the winter months. Adèle would also serve hot soup to customers who had braved the elements to attend a portrait sitting. Beyond this room was a large studio in which stood a tall tripod camera with traditional black material attached and from under which George would appear and make faces to encourage reluctant children to smile! Also in the studio were a seascape backdrop, an elaborate chair for formal sittings and many toys to occupy children, in whose portrait photography the firm specialised. Further to the rear of the premises was a small room, fitted out to store plateglass negatives; there were also two dark rooms. The couple and their four daughters lived over the shop. Dorothy, the eldest, was responsible for dressing the window. Routine tasks and general duties were carried out by Lily, a girl who worked for the Stones for many years.

Of the couple, George was the technical expert, the man who actually squeezed the rubber bulb on the cable releasing the shutter. He also developed and printed the films and acted as colourist if tinted photographs were required. Adèle, however, had the business head and dealt with enquiries, pricing and decision making. George, we understand, was perhaps too kindly and generous with money to be the financial controller of the partnership. He apparently had a fine singing voice and became very religious late in life. Adèle, who enjoyed spending time at her cottage in Painswick, had bright blue eyes and blonde hair, with a carefully maintained kiss-curl either side, to which her extravagantly decorated hats were pinned.

After George's death the business continued to be run by Adèle until she was in her eighties. She died in 1949 at the Stroud home of one of her daughters, at which point the business, which was one of the town's longer-established photographic concerns, ceased to exist.

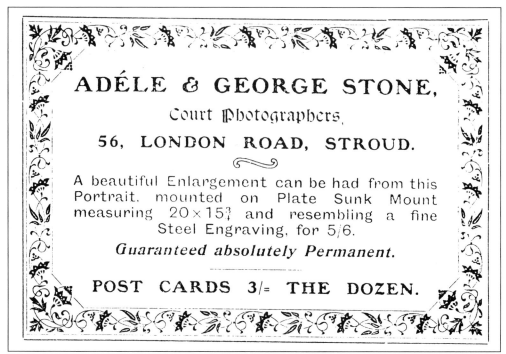

GEORGE AND ADELE STONE, PHOTOGRAPHERS. This is typical of the advertising labels used on the reverse of studio portraits prepared for customers.

THE BEARD FAMILY, c. 1910. William Beard (1875-1940), carpenter, the co-author's grandfather, stands at the rear door of his home in London Road, Stroud. With him are his wife Rosa and children Bert and Nellie (later Mrs. C.B.O. Smith).

PORTRAITS. The picture on the left, a cabinet-size photograph, is of an unidentified but delightful young lady. The right-hand portrait, a postcard, is apparently of a music teacher and was sent as a reminder of a forthcoming lesson. Signed E.B., it may well be from Miss Elsie Butcher, L.R.A.M., who, in January 1913, was advertising piano, violin and harmony lessons at her studio in Lansdown.

A HANDSOME COUPLE. There exist several portraits of the gentleman on the left, Mr H.T. Pearce, blacksmith, of London Road, Stroud. On this occasion he is partnered by another character dressed in a 'harem skirt', Mr Frank Ford. They often took part in local carnivals.

MARLING SCHOOL PRESENTATION. On his transfer from Uplands School to Marling, Charles Edward Shelton, born 1899, brought the number of pupils on roll to 100 for the first time. The event was marked, on 29 May 1912, with a presentation by Dr J.N. Frankland, Headmaster. The day selected for this ceremony was carefully chosen to coincide with the hundredth birthday of Mrs Mary Shelton, the boy's grandmother.

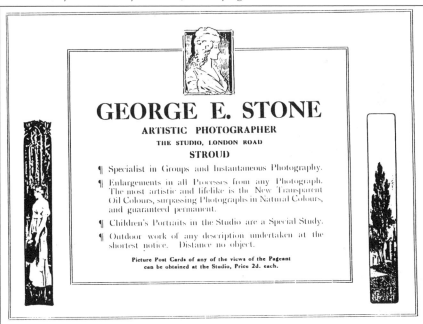

ADVERTISEMENT FOR GEORGE STONE, PHOTOGRAPHER. This insertion appeared in the pages of the Stroud Pageant Souvenir Booklet of 1911, which contained many of George Stone's photographs.

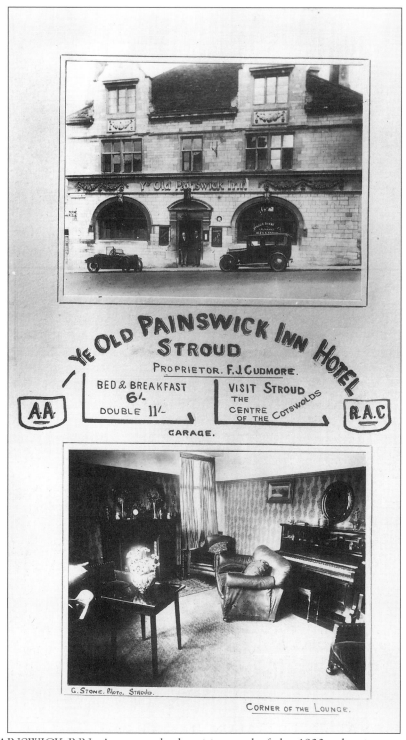

OLD PAINSWICK INN. An unusual advertising card of the 1930s, showing exterior and interior views of the hotel in lower Gloucester Street. It was obviously aimed at touring motorists, proclaiming Stroud to be 'the centre of the Cotswolds'.

EARLY MOTOR CLUB OUTING. This photograph was taken at the Horse Trough Junction at Ryeford, c. 1910. On the left, owned by Mr Godfrey of Lewis and Godfrey's drapery firm, is the Wolsley 'AD 850' driven by Tommy Reed, a salesman at Steel's garage in Stroud. He was later the town's first taxi driver. In the centre are a Darracq, AD 88, and a Talbot, AD 951. The Peugeot, AD 234, on the right, was owned and driven by Mr George Apperly of Rodborough Court. Supt. J. Biggs of Stroud Police is his front seat passenger.

G.W.R. BUSES AT STROUD STATION. These early motors were all manufactured by Milnes-Daimler. The differing body styles would be updated from time to time, to improve passenger comfort, using the same chassis. Services ran to outlying destinations such as Nailsworth, Painswick and Stonehouse.

THE EMPIRE PICTURE PLAYHOUSE. This cinema and theatre was given a 'bumper send-off' at its opening on Monday 17 February 1913. Following the projection of a picture of the king and the singing of The National Anthem, the audience was entertained by well-known artists R.T. Chinn, humorist, The Three Dines, vocalists, and Little Vera, child actress. The photograph shows the staff posing at the entrance to the foyer during the opening week.

THE EMPIRE AUDITORIUM. This view from the stage shows the traditional décor that would have greeted the 450 or so patrons it held. Seats were available at 3d, 6d and a shilling. A private box for four persons would cost six shillings. The building was replaced, in 1935, on the same site in London Road, by the Gaumont Palace Cinema. This subsequently became the Mecca Bingo Hall.

BLACKBIRD ON HER NEST. BUILT ON THE MANTLEPIECE IN LIVING ROOM. AT DUDBRIDGE, GLO'S.

STONE PHOTO, STROUD
COPYRIGHT.

THE DUDBRIDGE BLACKBIRD. The exploits of this little feathered celebrity caused much local interest in the spring of 1910. A pet of Samuel Hayden, it built its nest on the sitting room mantelpiece at Vale House near Dudbridge Corner. Having no mate, the resulting eggs did not hatch. After its owner had procured fertile eggs from two other nests the following year, the hen was able, as a single parent, to successfully rear her little brood. (See page 67.)

BLACKBIRDS NEST. BUILT ON MANTLEPIECE IN LIVING ROOM AT DUDBRIDGE. GLO'S

STONE PHOTO STROUD

COPYRIGHT.

THE HUSTINGS. C.P. Allen, M.P., stands at the back of a 1908 Peugeot driven by Mr Charles Apperly. (See page 70 for further references to this family.) This photograph was taken outside the Dudbridge Ironworks (now an architecturally modified Redlers) following the presentation of a yellow silk horseshoe by the firm's staff and a decorated boot from the foundry department. These tokens were to bring him good fortune in the two general elections that took place in 1910.

For . .

High-class
Photography

Lighting
and
Posing.

ADÈLE STONE, Artist,

56, London Road, STROUD.

C.P. ALLEN, ESQ, M.P. This portrait was taken following Allen's re-election in October 1910. He defeated C.A. Cripps, Conservative, in 1900 and held the Stroud Borough Constituency for the Liberals, often by a very narrow majority, until after the Great War. Election results were announced from the Subscription Rooms balcony , after which he would return to address his supporters from an upstairs window at the Liberal Club in Lansdown. (See page 62.) THE ADVERTISEMENT on the right is an early Adèle Stone example, suggesting the artistry that went into her work.

CASHES GREEN JAZZ BAND. This was one of the more eye-catching local bands that took part in the Stroud Hospital Effort carnival on Saturday 19 July 1924. In that year attempts were made to reduce the hospital's debts, due to recent building works, by organising events such as this. The heavy rain did little to dampen the spirits of those taking part, as the procession made its way from the hospital through the streets of Stroud to Fromehall Park.

Stone, Photo. Stroud.

CITY OF GLOUCESTER FIRE FLOAT, JULY 12TH 1906.

THE *SALAMANDER*. Built at Abdela and Mitchell's Boatyard at Hope Mill, Brimscombe, this fire-float was propelled by four water jets and was fitted with Merryweather fire pumps. It was subsequently stationed at Llanthony Bridge, Gloucester, in case required at the docks.

BUILT, ENGINED & DESIGNED BY I.J. ABDELA & MITCHELL Lᵀᴰ BRIMSCOMBE. ENGLAND.

THE S.L. *CALLARU* TOWING THE *ERENE*. The leading vessel, here being steered by Isaac J. Abdela himself, was 39 ft long, had a beam of 7 ft and a draught of 4 ft, displacing, in all, 7 tons. The 35 h.p. steam compound engine could propel the launch at 10 m.p.h. The *Erene* was a river barge constructed in steel. It is recorded that the vessels 'locked out' along the Thames and Severn Canal to London between 29 October and 2 November 1904. Their names suggest that they were probably destined for service in Northern Sri Lanka.

STROUD HOSPITAL, OPENING OF THE PEACE MEMORIAL WING. This took place on 6 July 1922. Seated to Matron's right is Princess Alice. Either side of them are Sir Percy and Lady Beatrice Marling. Other dignitaries included Major W.J.P. Marling, President of the hospital, the Bishop of Gloucester, Earl Beauchamp, Sir Ashton Lister, Mr A.W. Stanton, Canon Hawkins (Hospital Chaplain) and Mr Wood, architect.

CHRISTMAS AT STROUD HOSPITAL, 1921. Matron and her staff have dressed up to bring some festive cheer to the unusually large number of patients unable to go home for Christmas. Following a hearty lunch of turkey and plum pudding, gifts were distributed by the hospital president, after which all joined in carol singing with local church choirs. Each patient was also allowed two visitors with whom to share tea. (See also page 71.)

THE EXCELSIOR FOOTBALL TEAM, 1911-12. Their home ground was a breezy hilltop pitch above Fort St George, Rodborough. The second team, 'The Gothamites', and a third team also shared their facilities. A contemporary report of an away match at Swindon describes the team's performance on the day as 'muddling the ball and missing opportunities.' Players included Hampshire, Watson, Wager, Lovemore, Harrison, Beavis, Avens, Craig, Churchman, Kilmister and Gibbons.

CAUGHT IN HIS OWN TRAP. Speeding motorists have obviously been a problem since the advent of the automobile. This carnival entry was a lighthearted jest which amused the onlookers.

STROUD RUGBY CLUB, 1924-5 SEASON. This is one of a series of Rugby Club photographs which have survived. Many are preserved at the Club's headquarters at Fromehall Park. On the ground: W.G. Cole, T. Gough. Seated: H. Swayne (Vice Capt.), G. Durn, G. Edwards, C.A. Watkins (Capt.), F. Bennett, J. Phelps. Standing: P.L. Clissold (Match Secretary), J. Harris, F. Ashmead, R. Close, F. Stinchcombe, F. Whittaker (Trainer), M. Dudbridge, J.G. Buckley, F. Davis, H. Smith, H.C. Beck (Hon. Sec.).

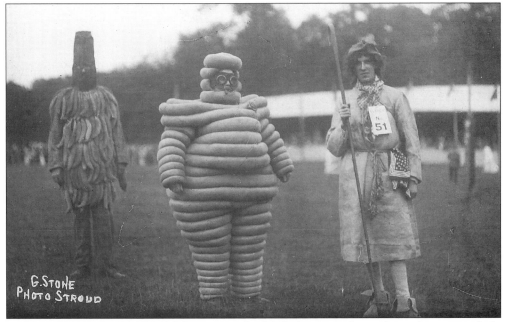

FANCY DRESS PARADE. Of this group, the Michelin man obviously made a particularly deep impression, since an elderly Stroud resident still recalls him after some 84 years.

CHILD IN A BOOT. This horse-drawn entry featured in a late Edwardian carnival trade section. Closer examination reveals that the exhibit was prepared by T.E. Revell and Son, family bootmakers, who had shops in Stroud High Street and in Bath.

GLOUCESTER STREET ARCH. It was an honour for Stroud to host the Gloucestershire Agricultural Society's shows in 1895, 1907 and again in June 1912, as shown here. Elaborate and artistically ingenious arches such as this example in Gloucester Street, were erected in various parts of the town and on the approach roads to the show site at Stratford Park. (See also pages 33, 58-60 and 106-7.)

Opposite, left: MR FRANK GWYNNE EVANS. This gentleman was secretary of the Pageant's organising committee and wrote the script. At the event's conclusion, the 1,000 plus performers, together with some 6,000 spectators, cheered in appreciation and respect. Proceeds went to Stroud Hospital and a police orphanage. Right: MISS MAY CULL. The Pageant Mistress, responsible for directing the performance's progress, is seen here holding the gold whistle and a bouquet of carnations and lilies which were presented to her by the performers.

Mid-Gloucestershire
Historical Pageant
of Progress

HELD AT

FROMEHALL PARK, STROUD
SATURDAY, SEPTEMBER 2nd
THURSDAY, SEPTEMBER 7th
SATURDAY, SEPTEMBER 9th

(Author, Frank Gwynne Evans)

Under the direction of MISS MAY E. CULL

HISTORICAL PAGEANT, 1911. This heading is taken from the official Pageant programme. Right: SARAH SIDDONS. This famous actress, played in the Pageant by Miss Gladys Waterer, featured in the eighteenth-century episode, acted out by the residents of Cainscross, Cashes Green, Ebley, Randwick and Whiteshill. (See also pages 68 and 69.)

'SPOT'. Mr Vincent Walker, manager of the Electric Photo-Play House in Lansdown, is seen here dressed in African costume, together with his helpers, Timbuc-One and Timbuc-Two.

'SPOT' AGAIN. On this occasion Mr Walker wears an elaborate Red Indian costume for another carnival appearance.

ADVERTISEMENT FOR THE PHOTOPLAY HOUSE, 1911. This appeared near the end of the Pageant programme.

Have you ever heard of the ELECTRIC Photo-Play House?

E V E R Y E V E N I N G 7.30 ; Saturday, 3, 7 and 9.

Manager : VINCENT WALKER   Telephone 228

It is really very comfortable. Cool in Summer, Cosy and Warm in Winter.

Our Photo-Plays are changed Monday and Thursday.

We exhibit none but the Latest and Best of the World's productions. The Programmes are Refined and always up-to-date. If anything should happen, you can always see it at Photo-Play House.

The ELECTRIC
Photo-Play House
(Lansdown, Stroud).

BALCONY (Special Reserved Seats)	-	-	-	-	1/6
BALCONY -	-	-	-	-	1/-
BACK SEATS -	-	-	-	-	9d.
BODY OF HALL	-	-	-	6d. and 3d.	

WASPS' NEST. Sometimes people, fascinated by the symmetry, size and structure of these insect homes, had them professionally photographed, as in the case of this example. The location of the nest is unidentified.

LIPTON, LTD. This shop was situated at 65 High Street, next to Revell's shoe shop. It was just one of several provision merchants situated in this busy thoroughfare. A variety of produce is clearly displayed and priced, such as sliced bacon at 2d per pound. The open air meat display is a far cry from the requirements of today's health and hygiene regulations.

Three
Henry J. Comley

Henry John Comley was born on 13 August 1868 at Graham Street, Newport, Monmouthshire, son of Henry Comley and his wife Ann, née Tanner. His father, a ship's chief officer, later a Master Mariner, was dead by 1890 when Henry junior married Alice Reed at Newport Register Office. A daughter, Gladys Claretta Valorita, was born in 1893. She married a man with equally resonant forenames, Clarence Goff Wolfe Lovemore, at St Bartholomew's, Bristol in 1919.

HENRY J. COMLEY, F.R.P.S. This promotional photograph was taken around 1900.

Sometime around 1902 Henry J. Comley moved to Gloucestershire in order to take over the business of Stroud photographer J.H. Elliott at 10 Russell Street. Comley was a Fellow of the Royal Photographic Society, the holder of some forty awards and a Gold Medallist, as his trade cards announced. He appears to have wished to impress the town by renaming his premises The County Studio. He remained in Stroud for some twenty years, apparently selling out to E.O. Reynolds around 1922. By 1927 the firm was owned by W. Dennis Moss and Peckham. From 1931 it was in the sole hands of Edwin C. Peckham and continues as a photographic business to the present day, still operating under Peckham's name, though after a succession of owners. A decorative guttering above the shop indicates that the building was put up in 1893 (Elliott's former premises were in George Street and Union Street as early as 1889) so it is interesting to note that a photographic business has been conducted out of the same building in Russell Street for over a century. Advertisements in various directories show that, in addition to standard developing, printing and enlarging services, Comley also published 'Views of the neighbourhood in great variety' (many of which are reproduced for the first time in this book) and offered an information and advice service for amateur photographers. His publicity also mentions paintings in oils and water colours, cameras, plates, films, papers, developers, etc.

Where Comley settled after leaving Stroud is uncertain, though his wife, Alice, died at a house in Barnwood Road, Gloucester, in 1936. At the time of his death from bronchitis and heart disease on 6 March 1953 at Penylan, Cardiff, he was described as a retired photographic artist. He left his estate, worth £4286 17s 10d to his daughter Gladys.

Comley's output was varied. During the twenty years he was in business in Stroud he produced a huge quantity of portraits and a relatively small number of real photographic landscape postcards, notably of Minchinhampton Common, Burleigh and Randwick. His principal claim to fame lies in his coverage of carnivals, elections and especially of the 1911 Historical Pageant of Progress, staged at Fromehall Park. His postcards have no continuous serial numbers but are usually identified by a stamp, including his name, impressed into the card. Comley's plate glass negatives have, sadly, not survived, unlike those of his successor, E.C. Peckham.

Two examples of Comley's portraiture.

ADVERTISEMENT. This is how Comley chose to publicise his business in an Edwardian
directory.

AGRICULTURAL SHOW, 1907. Town youngsters pose under the George Street arch, constructed just below the Wilts and Dorset Bank, whose manager at this period bore the impressive sounding name of Theodore Lovell de Behr. The arch is particularly rich in bunting and greenery. It was some fifteen years since the County Agricultural Show had visited Stroud and the town was clearly determined to do the occasion justice. Note also the Victorian gas-lamps. (See the following page and also pages 33, 50, 60 and 106-7.)

AGRICULTURAL SHOW FLOAT, 1907. The message on the reverse of this postcard states that the float, which was awarded fourth prize, was driven by Mr Malpass, and that the children included Lucy Prout, Nellie Dixon, Hilda Gwinnell, Bob Dee, Charlie Poole, Evelett Malpass, Albert Cook, Lily Smith and Ivy Philips. Clothing consisted of sacking and brown calico, helped along with earth paints and feathers. The wigwam was supported by a young larch tree. The cart trimmings were hay and larch leaves. Suddenly changing the subject, the writer concludes, apparently with unintended humour, that the scouts have had to be disbanded as the Rector 'could not carry on without a woman'. (See also pages 33, 50, 58, 60 and 106-7.)

DECORATED ARCH, STATION ROAD, STROUD, 1912. As this postcard reveals, arches were erected to celebrate shows and carnivals on several occasions before the First World War. (See pages 33, 50, 58, 59 and 106.) In this picture, posters on the station wall advertise G.W.R. trips to Ireland. The postcard, sent by their daughter to a Mr and Mrs Lloyd at Westcliff-on-Sea, includes the quaint message, 'Thank you ever so much for the jam. We are going for a picnic in some most lovely woods and are taking a pot.'

DRAKE'S COMET, JANUARY 1910. As Comley's inscription makes clear, this postcard represents a combination of his artistic and photographic skills. The local press reported that the comet was seen quite clearly in many parts of Britain, from Oban to Dover, where it 'came suddenly into view just over the western heights a little before six. It looked brighter than ever, like a great lamp in the sky.'

LAYING THE CORNERSTONE, UPLANDS CHURCH, 1908. The ceremony of laying the foundation stone of the new church of All Saints' at Uplands on 30 June 1908, was performed by Viscount St Aldwyn in the presence of a large crowd, including many local dignitaries and schoolchildren from Uplands and Slad. (See page 21.) Newspaper reports record that the weather was perfect and that a bottle containing newspapers and a current coin of the realm was placed in a cavity beneath the stone.

UPLANDS, GENERAL VIEW. This picture shows the church already built, though the tower and spire were not added until some twenty years later.

DECLARATION OF POLL, STROUD SUBSCRIPTION ROOMS, 1910. This crowded scene depicts the moment when C.P. Allen was returned as Liberal Member for Stroud in the January General Election of that year. (The country was called to vote again in December.) Under its heading of 'Unprecedented Enthusiasm', the *Stroud Journal* described the occasion as follows:

'The votes recorded on Wednesday for the election of a Parliamentary representative for the Stroud Division of Gloucestershire were counted at the Subscription Rooms, Stroud, on Thursday morning,the count commencing at 10.30. About midday a huge crowd assembled in the open space outside the Rooms – Kendrick Street, Bedford Street and George Street being packed with people. Party colours were very prominent and the enclosed space near the entrance to the Rooms was occupied by the members of the Stroud club and their friends. Election songs appertaining to both parties were sung over and over again, whilst cheers and counter-cheers were given for Mr Allen and Mr Clifford. The utmost good humour prevailed and the police arrangements (under Supt. Biggs) were admirable. As 12.30 was reached, the crowd became anxious and, as the poll was declared in 1906 at 12.45, there was great exuberance and anxiety when that hour had passed. It was felt certain that the poll would be heavy and this accounted for the delay in the declaration. At five minutes past one, Mr Twitchett, the caretaker of the Rooms, appeared on the balcony and spread a piece of red cloth on the table in readiness for the candidates to appear, but he gave no sign whatever to indicate the state of the figures. Excitement now ran very high and at 1.15 the window was thrown up and it was at once evident that Mr Allen, being on the right side of the Returning Officer, was 'in'. Great cheers were raised and both Mr Allen and Mr Clifford smiled pleasantly at the dense crowd. Inside the room Mr Clifford took his defeat like a thorough gentleman. Naturally he was disappointed, but he shook hands with Mr Allen and heartily congratulated him upon his victory. In addition to the officials, Sir Alfred Apperly (the local leader of the Liberal party),

WILLIAM BURTON STEWART. This gentleman, who lived at Ebley Court, was C.P. Allen's defeated Conservative opponent in the 1906 General Election. 'Roll on, Charlie Allen,' was one of the Liberal slogans during several campaigns. As a counter to this, it is reported that the Conservatives published a cartoon with Allen rolling down Cam Peak in a barrel labelled, 'One-sided Free Trade' and 'Home Rule', while Mr Burton Stewart was shown standing underneath the British Flag at the summit. Elections were certainly spirited occasions in Edwardian days.

CECIL E. FITCH. At the second General Election of 1910, Charles Allen was once more victorious, though with a reduced majority of 202, this time over Cecil Fitch. Like Clifford, Fitch, it is recorded, 'took his defeat splendidly, smiled pleasantly and waved to the crowd.' An idea of election rhetoric at this period may be gauged from the following: Allen announced that they had 'whacked 'em for the fourth time and could go on whacking them for ever.'

Major Ricardo (the Conservative leader), Messrs G.E. Harrison (Liberal Agent) and George Scriven (Conservative Agent) were on the balcony. Mr E.P. Little (the Returning Oficer) had the figures ready to hang over the balcony as follows: C.P. Allen (L) 5,285; A.W. Clifford (C) 4,962; Liberal majority 323. Further information about C.P. Allen may be found on page 45.

What do I care about the Election?

As long as I am sitting in one of Wilkes' fine, comfortable Easy Chairs, I simply can't, and I won't worry about anything. I feel far too snug and happy to let Elections bother me. I'll vote all right when the time comes—but till then, leave me alone with my good old chair. It's my best chum,

SHERATON HOUSE ANNUAL FURNISHING SALE
Commenced JANUARY 14th, for 14 Days only.

J.H. WILKES.

SHERATON HOUSE, STROUD

'Phone 133.

WILKES' ADVERTISEMENT, JANUARY 1910. This amusing advertisement appeared in the local press at the time of C.P. Allen's contest with A.W. Clifford.

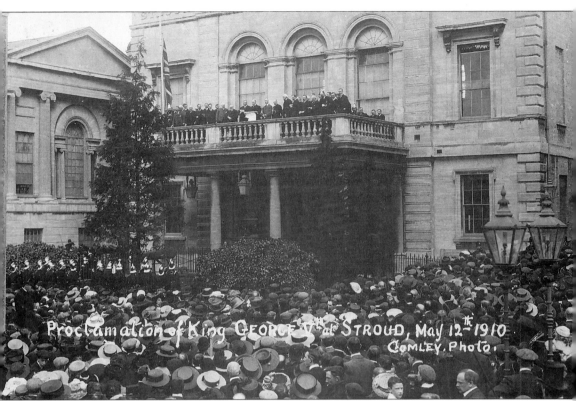

Proclamation of King George Vth at STROUD, May 12th 1910.
COMLEY. Photo.

PROCLAMATION OF KING GEORGE V, 12 May 1910. Following the rather sudden death of Edward VII, the new king was proclaimed to the citizens of Stroud from the Subscription Rooms balcony by Mr G.W. Godsell, Urban District Council Chairman. The two fire brigades, Urban and Volunteer, were present, under their respective captains Tanner and Ford, and Mr R. Knight sounded a trumpet fanfare. Punctually at 1.15 p.m., Mr F. Miles, Clerk in the Council Office, announced Mr Godsell's presence with the words, 'Oyez! oyez! oyez! All persons are required to keep silence, whilst the King's Proclamation is openly read, upon pain of imprisonment.' When the reading of the Proclamation was complete, another trumpet fanfare followed and the National Anthem, in a version by Mr John White of George Street, was sung. The short ceremony concluded with Mr Godsell calling for three cheers for King George and Queen Mary, which were 'royally given with much heartiness'.

STROUD BREWERY, DECORATED FOR THE CORONATION OF 1911. The headquarters building of the Stroud Brewery Company in Rowcroft was liberally festooned with flags and bunting to celebrate the coronation of George V. Note the public weighbridge on the right.

THE CORONATION PROCESSION: STROUD FIREMEN. Henry Comley took many photographs of this important occasion. Here firemen, the more senior with epaulettes, assemble on King Street Parade. Note the white gloves tucked into their belts.

THE DUDBRIDGE BLACKBIRDS. This picture, also taken at the Coronation Carnival, shows a float complete with nest and blackbirds. This indicates the extent to which the nest on the mantelpiece at Dudbridge had already passed into popular folklore. This float, staged by Miss Adèle Stone, the photographer, alludes to the much publicized nest built by a blackbird on the mantelpiece at Mr Hayden's house at Dudbridge. As the *Stroud Journal* records, 'A wagon bore a huge nest of hay and three little boys as "blackbirds" popped up and down. Mr Samuel Hayden would have been bound to admit that it was a good representation of his feathered companions.' (See page 43.)

CARNIVAL BOAT. This unusual entry was the work of Holy Trinity Church.

THE PAGEANT OF PROGRESS, 1911. Details of the authorship and organization of the pageant can be found in the section of the book concerning George and Adèle Stone. (See page 51.) In this photograph, participants, mostly from villages in the Nailsworth valley and Minchinhampton, portray episode 2 of the pageant, set in 1050 AD and entitled, 'Godwin and Gytha'.

THE PAGEANT OF PROGRESS, QUEEN ELIZABETH AND HUGUENOT REFUGEES (EPISODE V) AD 1574. The performers in this, perhaps the most lovely and splendidly costumed scene, hailed from Stroud, Uplands and Rodborough. The setting is a Cloth Fair, with maypole dancing and pedlars hawking their wares. The Sheriff announces the arrival of the Queen, Miss Seymour Keay (Pageant Mistress of the Robes), who is presented with a roll of cloth by the head of the Weavers' Guild, Charles A. Apperly (whose family owned the ground and were long-established woollen manufacturers). Finally, on come the Huguenot refugees, who are roughly treated by the crowd until the Queen promises them her protection.

THE PAGEANT OF PROGRESS. Queen Elizabeth I was played by Miss Seymour Keay of Minchinhampton.

CARNIVAL PROCESSION, RUSSELL STREET. The occasion of this splendid crowd scene remains uncertain, but the picture is full of life and interest. Note, on the left, the premises of Walter Wells, jeweller, and, next door, with a horse's head shop sign, that of John Pearce, sadler.

Floral Tributes at the Funeral of Sir Alfred Apperly. Sept. 1913.

FLORAL TRIBUTES TO SIR ALFRED APPERLY. Sir Alfred, of the Dudbridge firm of Messrs Apperly, Curtis and Co. Ltd, founded by his grandfather, died on 7 September 1913 at his home, Rodborough Court. Sir Alfred, a prominent local Liberal, had been responsible, in 1895, for introducing C.P. Allen to the constituency. Sir Alfred was knighted in 1907. As President of the Stroud Volunteer Fire Service, he was instrumental in acquiring for the brigade a new modern steam fire engine. (See page 44 for a reference to Sir Alfred's son, Charles.)

STROUD HOSPITAL, c. 1910. In this fine, detailed photograph, the men's ward is decorated with Chinese lanterns, vases and greenery. Several nurses appear to have entered into the spirit of the occasion by dressing up in oriental costume. (See also page 47.)

CHUBBY. Stroud Hospital must surely have benefitted from the fundraising assistance of such a winning canine helper.

FIRE AT TOWNSEND'S MILL. This corn and seed business at Stratford Mill, on the site now occupied by Tesco's store, burned down in a disastrous fire on 15 June 1908. Rebuilt, it later suffered a further conflagration before piecemeal demolition to make way for Tesco's store.

FIRE AT COOPER'S HILL. Situated at Beeches Green, Cooper's Hill was the residence of Mr Lloyd, a retired wine merchant, his wife and three daughters. The house caught fire in February 1905 and was gutted. Both fire engines attended and there were several narrow escapes, including that of two servant girls who, finding their access stairs ablaze, were helped by the cook to safety along coping stones and a narrow ledge. Damage from the blaze was estimated at £2,000, a sizeable sum for those days.

FIRE AT RODBOROUGH MANOR. This mansion, the home of Judge Ellicott, caught fire on 28 August 1906. The blaze was believed to have originated in the billiard room. Compare, on page 96, W.F. Lee's view of the aftermath.

STORM DAMAGE, BOWBRIDGE POST OFFICE, JANUARY 1906. The same storm that felled the trees in Beard's Lane (see page 98) led to a fatal accident at Bowbridge. Miss Ethel Butt, 25, a telegraphist and the postmaster's daughter, was killed when, at 6.20 a.m., a 12 ft chimneystack fell on the bed (right) where she was sleeping. Her sister Myrtle, who was in the same bed, and another sister miraculously escaped uninjured. An estimated three tons of rubble and a beam fell on Ethel who, perhaps not surprisingly, died shortly after being extricated.

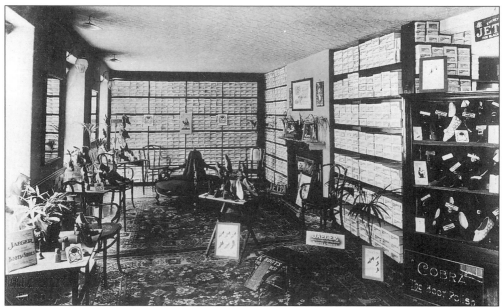

SHOE SHOP INTERIOR, STROUD. The reverse of this postcard reads, 'Thought perhaps you would like a card of our ladies' fitting room.' Exactly which shoe shop this refers to is unclear, though Revell's, of 66 and 67 High Street, is a strong possibility. The store stocked, amongst other brands, shoes by Jaeger and Lotus. Note the stylish circular seat at the rear of the picture.

Lotus

Take the same pains to be fitted with Lotus as you would when getting a pair of shoes made to measure. Keep trying pairs on until you get a perfect fit; there are plenty of sizes and widths in Lotus.

Ladies' Shoe

Ladies' Shoe No **92** New style.

12/9

per pair for cash.

Strong sole shoe for hard wear in town or country. Comfortable and reliable.

Milward's

Stroud and County Boot Stores......... 59, High St, Stroud.

SHOE SHOP ADVERTISEMENT. Milward's also stocked Lotus shoes. Their fitting room offers another possible location for the photograph above.

74

TRAIN TRIP TO LONDON, 1910. Sponsored and arranged by the *Stroud News*, a train excursion to London to see the Japanese Exhibition at Uxbridge Road took place in July 1910. Some 600 people took advantage of this opportunity to visit the Capital, the train also picking up at Stonehouse, Brimscombe and Chalford. The upper picture shows the crowd arriving in the Station Yard, the lower one the departure. Although it hardly seems so from the lower picture, the *Stroud News* reporter recorded his amusement at several passengers' modest efforts to avoid being caught by Comley on film. The excursion returned to Stroud at 3.30 a.m. next morning. (See also page 102.)

LAUNDRY INTERIOR. These photographs were taken inside a laundry believed to have been situated in buildings at the bottom of what is now called Libby's Drive, off Slad Road in Stroud. The initials on the baskets prove it was a branch of the Gloucester Model Laundry Ltd. The lady in the arch in the lower picture is Miss Winifred Clarke of Bowbridge Lane.

MOTORCYCLE AND SIDECAR. Mr Albert Waite, nearest the top of the picture, was a pioneering motor mechanic in the Stroud area, one of the first people to own a motorcycle. The photographs were taken in 1912, the lower one showing a specially adapted sidecar, fitted with cup trays and intended to hold eggs collected from local farms. A message in Mr Waite's own hand records that he personally designed the chassis and fittings. In the lower picture, the machine, a new B.S.A. 4 Qr h.p. 2 speed free engine model, is seen on test in Field Road, Stroud, with F.M. Smith and A. Marsh (in boaters) and a traveller on board.

WYCLIFFE COLLEGE, STONEHOUSE. In this graceful postcard study, franked in 1920, some ten years after the event it records, stalls and a public address system (left) have been set up in the school grounds. A cryptic message on the reverse, written by F.H. Sherwell, music master at the school for some forty years, reads, 'Gratias agimus tibi.' (We give thee thanks).

PROCESSION, HOLY TRINITY CHURCH, STROUD. In this picture, taken around 1910, the photographer catches the attention of a small boy watching a procession pass up Trinity Road.

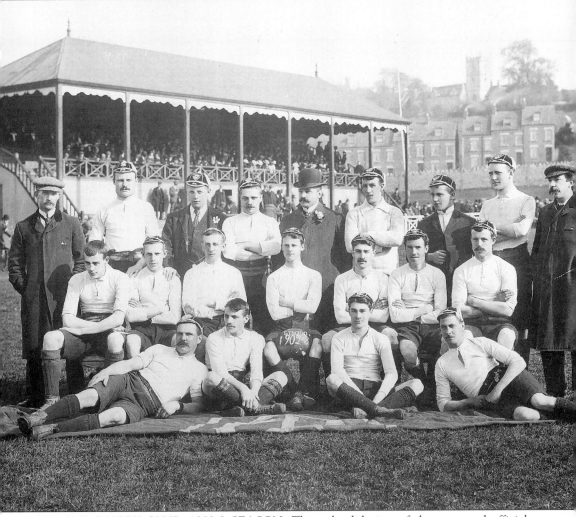

STROUD RUGBY CLUB, 1902-3 SEASON. This splendid view of the team and officials shows, in the background, the Club's impressive wooden stand in Fromehall Park. The caption also mentions that this had been a season of record success for Stroud. Those pictured are, back row: J.T. Curtis (Match Secretary), F.W. Harrison, G. Matthews, J. Whiley, Dr Crosby (President), G. Fowke, A. Brown, J. Matthews, F. Wheatley (Hon. Sec.). Middle row: H. Chew (Vice Capt.), W.J. Kibblewhite, L. Smith, B. Blanch (Capt.), T.W. Cull, S. Blanch, W. Partridge. Front row: W. Shewell, F. Brown, W.S. Cull, H. Smith.

BRIMSCOMBE A.F.C., 1903. A caption above the original photograph records that this team won the 1902-3 District League Cup. Back row: E. Budding (linesman), P. Kimmins, A. Hampton, W. James (secretary) H. Dickenson. Middle row: F. Hook, W. Aldridge, G. Emblin (capt.), D. Peyton, J. Shewell, H. Poole. Front row: A. Rowle, F. Roberts. F. Johnson, F. Munday. Interestingly, the photograph was taken by Comley whilst working for J. H. Elliott, before the former took over the firm in his own right.

BRADSHAW'S SHOP, HIGH STREET, STROUD. By around 1910, when this photograph was taken, James Bradshaw had opened his business in Stroud. 'Cheapest shop in the town,' he proclaims above the door – also, arguably, the most varied, since he sold fruit, flowers, seeds, vegetables, fish – including oysters – and ice. Mr Bradshaw's shop stood where Cornhill now joins the top of the High Street.

Four
William F. Lee

The portrait below, taken around 1902, marks the beginning of the period in his career when Lee worked as a photographer in Stroud.

W.F.Lee was born in Cardiff on 2nd September 1886, third son of James Lee, a printer by trade, and Annie Eliza, née Wheadon. Both his parents were born at Bridport on the Dorset coast. In 1891, when William was five, the family moved to Stroud, where James opened a stationer's business at 29 High Street.

WILLIAM FREDERICK LEE.

William Lee was educated at Castle Street and Parliament Street Primary Schools before winning, in 1898, a scholarship to the local Grammar School, recently founded by Sir Samuel Marling. It is known that by 1900 the school boasted a thriving photographic club where it is very probable that Lee acquired his skill with the camera.

In 1902, because of the new Post Office regulations referred to earlier, Lee suddenly found himself in an ideal position to exploit the booming demand for picture postcards: he himself had the necessary photographic skills, while his father was a printer with a shop from which to retail the finished product.

Lee was only sixteen when his first postcards were published. Some views – those which appeared in printed postcard form – were fairly run-of-the-mill but, in his Photographic Series, Lee really came into his own. Well over 200 of these real photographic postcards have survived. Mostly they are accurately focussed, clear and well composed: they chronicle in fascinating detail the events, pastimes and village life of the first decade of this century. Foregrounds are well peopled with workmen, traders and children in their everyday garb, going about their day-to-day business. Lee's work is objective, yet sensitive and important for the social historian.

Around 1911 W.F.Lee concluded his partnership with his father, left Stroud to work as a traveller for a London stationer's firm and wound up his career as a photographer. He was 25.

W.F. Lee's work took him to Northern Ireland. There, at Portrush, he met his future wife, Rachel Pepper. They married in 1912 and opened a stationer's and picture-framing business in Cheltenham. Apart from a few snow scenes, almost no postcards can be attributed to him during the forty years or so he ran his business in Winchcombe Street. William and Rachel retired about 1950, stayed in the town another decade or so and finally moved to Kingswood, Bristol, to be near their younger daughter. Lee died on Christmas Day 1965 in his eightieth year; his wife passed away a few months later.

JAMES LEE. James, W.F. Lee's father, was born at Bridport, Dorset, in 1856, son of Elijah Lee, captain of a coastal sailing vessel curiously named the Whynot. James was apprenticed as a printer, working for some years in Cardiff before settling around 1891 in Stroud, where his elder brother, Frederick Thomas (the writer's great-grandfather) ran a tailor's business. From a third brother, William Joseph, descends the more celebrated Lee family of Slad. James eventually returned to his home town, where he died in 1937.

THE TOP OF THE HIGH STREET, STROUD. On the left of this busy street scene is the shop which Lee's father, James, ran for some thirty-six years and where his son developed and printed his photographs.

LEE BROTHERS, STATIONER'S REPRESENTATIVES. This promotional postcard was issued during the time when W.F. Lee and his brothers, Sydney and Albert, worked together as travelling salesmen for a London stationery firm.

TROLLEY ACCIDENT, STROUD HIGH STREET. Lee didn't have far to go to record this mishap, which seems to have attracted a great deal of public interest: his father's shop can be seen on the left of the picture. Note the working clothes of most of the bystanders, also the rams' heads above the pillars on Williams' butchers shop next door.

STREET TRADERS, HIGH STREET, STROUD. The traders' trucks, selling fish, fruit and vegetables, were a feature of old Stroud and are still remembered by elderly residents. From a social history standpoint it is worth noting that a flower-seller operates today from almost exactly the same spot. This is one of Lee's more important pictures.

RUSSELL STREET, STROUD. In this view of around 1909, the shops are of interest. Ricketts' confectioner's premises and The Bricklayer's Arms mark the position of Hurran's lately vacated shop. Freeman's, beyond, is now an estate agent's. The pub on the right sells Brimscombe Brewery Ales. Note the splendid gas-lamps and the post office delivery boy posing in the road.

KENDRICK STREET, STROUD. This street was rarely photographed, so views of it are all the more significant when discovered. At the far end, the pedimented building is Withey's grocery store, a long-established concern, with Bell's drapery shop adjoining. On the right, the staff of Fletcher's butchery business watch the photographer.

ROWCROFT, STROUD. The fine iron and glass portico on the left has not survived; neither have the tree and the building far right, with its placards advertising bargains to be had at Baker's picture-framing premises. When this photograph was taken, George Holloway's statue was only a decade or so old.

C.B. GARDNER'S SHOP. Occupying a prime position on the corner of High Street and King Street, Gardner's, hatters and milliners, can be traced back to around 1850. This photograph was taken in 1909, as the sale poster in the window proves.

King Street. Stroud. Sept 1900

Rec⁴ J W Sale

Bo.ᵗ of C. B. Gardner,

Hatter, Hosier, Glover,

SHIRT AND COLLAR MAKER.

Aug 16	Dressing silk hat			6
20	4 Collars	6/-	2	2
28	2 —	6d	1	1
.	½ dz —		4	
Sep 11	Sweater		3	
	2 Ties	1/3	2	6
	½ doz Handkerchiefs		5	3
			18	6

Paid
C B Gardner
Sep¹ 12/01

GARDNER'S BILL. In 1900 Revd T.W. Sale of Brownshill Court, Slad, bought collars for 6 Q w d at Gardner's shop. He had his silk hat dressed for 6d and purchased a surprisingly modern-sounding sweater for 3s.

MULVANY'S HAIRDRESSING SALON. In the window of Arthur Mulvany's shop at 7 King Street are displayed a host of lotions, potions and toilet requisites. The proprietor himself, surely of Irish origin, stands in the doorway. Newspaper advertisements for this business refer to 'Marcel Waving' and manicure.

THE ALMSHOUSES, CHURCH STREET. It could be argued that the demolition of these fine almshouses constitutes one of Stroud's more important post-war architectural losses. The old Vicarage, now Church Court Nursing Home, can be seen in the background, with the church itself on the left.

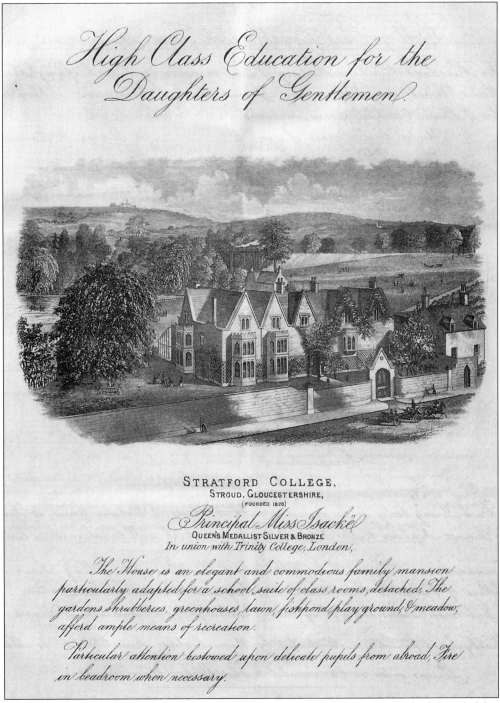

High Class Education for the Daughters of Gentlemen.

STRATFORD COLLEGE,
STROUD, GLOUCESTERSHIRE,
(FOUNDED 1820)

Principal Miss Isacke
QUEEN'S MEDALLIST SILVER & BRONZE
In union with Trinity College, London,

The House is an elegant and commodious family mansion particularly adapted for a school, suite of class rooms, detached. The gardens shrubberies, greenhouses, lawn, fishpond, play ground, & meadow, afford ample means of recreation.

Particular attention bestowed upon delicate pupils from abroad, Fire in bedroom when necessary.

STRATFORD ABBEY COLLEGE PROSPECTUS. In 1828 James Isacke had founded his brush manufacturing business which was run, around 1900, from premises in Church Street. His daughter, Rosa Stella, was Principal of Stratford Abbey College, which, as this leaflet of 1885 shows, catered for the more well-to-do young ladies of the district. This early building, enlarged in 1699, was demolished in 1961; the site is now Tesco's car park.

KING STREET PARADE, STROUD, A SNOWY SCENE. In this Edwardian view the Victoria Rooms can be seen far left, with The Royal George Hotel beyond. Lewis and Godfrey's store was, for many years, the town's largest drapery concern.

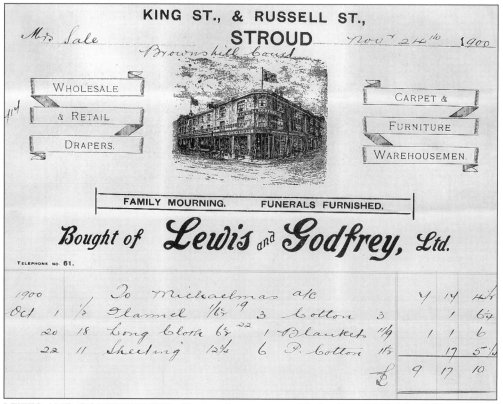

LEWIS AND GODFREY'S BILL. During the quarter to Michaelmas 1900, Mrs Sale, widow of the aforementioned clergyman, had run up a draper's bill for nearly £8. In October various purchases took her account to £9 17s 10d. The firm had to wait a further half-year for payment.

CASTLE PITCH, A PRETTY SNOW VIEW. W.F. Lee enjoyed taking his camera out in wintry weather, as this second seasonal picture shows. Here postmen empty the pillarbox at the lower end of the pitch which joins London Road to Castle Street. The Castle in question was, of course, the home of Stroud's long-lived historian, Paul Hawkins Fisher (1779-1873).

THE OLD TOWN HALL, STROUD. One of a limited number of Tudor buildings which
survive in Stroud, the Old Town Hall also housed the Urban District Council fire engine,
whose ladders and turntable are clearly visible.

WALLBRIDGE, c. 1910. This is an interesting photograph of a little-recorded part of Stroud. Several buildings shown here have disappeared, for instance The Ship Inn (left foreground) whose landlord was John Lee – no relation to the photographer. Note the Stroud Brewery buildings and chimney, visible above The Ship and, far left, the pediment of the Canal Company's headquarters. Hill Paul's clothing factory is prominent on the right of the picture. A milk delivery boy lingers at the kerbside.

FOLLY LANE, STROUD. A fine Victorian gas-lamp dominates the Beeches Green entrance to Folly Lane. The Catholic Church is in the background. The tall railings on the left have gone and the lane off to the right is now called Loveday's Mead. Note the unmetalled road surface.

MIDDLE STREET, STROUD. This photograph would appear to have been taken outside the house now numbered 73.

PRIMITIVE METHODIST CHAPEL, PARLIAMENT STREET. The Methodist cause in Stroud was founded in 1763. The Primitive Methodist Chapel, a much later offshoot, was described in 1910 as seating 400, though the size of such a modest building would suggest something of a crush! For some years now the chapel, converted and extended, has served as the town's only permanent theatre, The Cotswold Playhouse.

SLAD ROAD AND THE UPLANDS. In this detailed scene, Nathaniel Baxter's builder's yard is in the foreground. Note the wooden frames used in arch construction. The site is now occupied by Stroud Creamery. On the left is the Hound Brand clothing business. This building later housed Baughan's motorcycle factory.

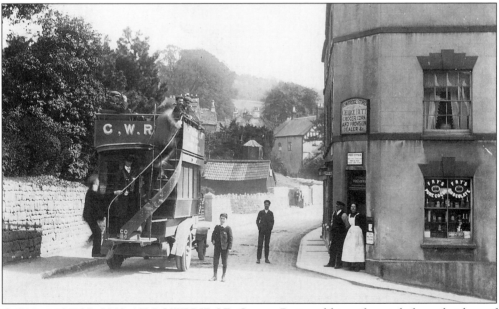

G.W.R. MOTOR BUS AT BOWBRIDGE. George Butt and his wife watch from the door of their Post Office stores as passengers hurry up the outside steps of the Stroud to Chalford G.W.R. Motor Bus. The relatively long exposure required for this picture has left the figures blurred. (It was the Butts' daughter who was killed by falling masonry in the great storm of January 1906; see pages 73 and 98.)

THE TURNPIKE, BUTTERROW. The old turnpike house was a shop in 1907 when this photograph was taken. The toll board which, in its restored form, shows the scale of charges for various vehicles and animals, then bore the name of John Willis, licensed dealer in tobacco and snuff. (Compare the photograph on page 114.) The Woolpack Inn can be seen in the lane beyond, with the little Methodist Chapel below, on the hill leading down to Bowbridge.

RODBOROUGH MANOR FIRE. On 28 August 1906 a disastrous fire broke out in the billiard room of Judge Ellicott's home. This is one of several pictures taken by Lee showing the aftermath of the blaze. The gentleman in the doorway and the ladies with parasols are probably the owner and his family. The furniture that was rescued occupies the foreground. (See also page 73.)

VINERY TEA ROOMS, RODBOROUGH FORT. Fort St George, as Rodborough Fort was known in 1910, boasted, amongst other attractions, a teahouse. In this view of its interior, a placard announces that the tower is open to visitors.

RODBOROUGH FORT, 1904. The inner courtyard of the building is much less frequently photographed than its exterior. Here a group of schoolgirls pays a visit to the Fort, which functioned as a private hotel and pleasure gardens. Its proprietress was Mrs Mary Tuck, who may well be one of the ladies in the doorway. (See also pages 116 and 117.)

STORM DAMAGE, JANUARY 1906. During the early hours of 6 January 1906 a savage storm struck the Stroud district. Within an area one mile long by 400 yards wide, upwards of forty mature trees were blown down or broken. This was the same storm which struck Bowbridge Post Office with such tragic results. (See page 73.) Here local children pose in the branches of one of three large trees which fell in Beard's Lane, off Cainscross Road.

PAGANHILL LANE, CAINSCROSS. This view of around 1905 shows the Spring Inn on the left. The stream which passes under the road in the centre of the picture rejoices in the name of Cuckold's Brook. The road level has now been raised.

CUP MANIA. This delightfully unposed photograph was taken in the field below Stroud General Hospital, the site now occupied by the Maternity Hospital. On Saturday 18 March 1905 Dursley won the Mid-Gloucestershire League Rugby Football Cup, donated and presented by M.P. Charles Allen. Only a few minutes after the final whistle, records the *Stroud News*, the result was 'ticked over the telegraph wires and displayed in a shop window in Dursley'. When the winning team finally arrived home, the Volunteer Band struck up 'See the Conquering Hero' and captain Tommy Atkins, flourishing the cup, was carried shoulder-high through the town.

LOCAL CHILDREN, RANDWICK. The photographer captures the interest of three village children pictured below the Vinetree Inn, which is seen top right.

RUSCOMBE CHAPEL, c. 1910. Local youngsters pose against the railings in front of the Congregational Chapel, founded in 1828 and enlarged by the addition of a Sunday School room a century later. Two of them carry baskets and are probably delivery boys.

VILLAGERS, RUSCOMBE. In this interesting photograph, important for reasons of social history, local people gather, as in the previous picture, to collect water and to gossip. Both the boy on the right and two of his companions have buckets to fill at the nearby spring.

VILLAGERS, RUSCOMBE (DETAIL).

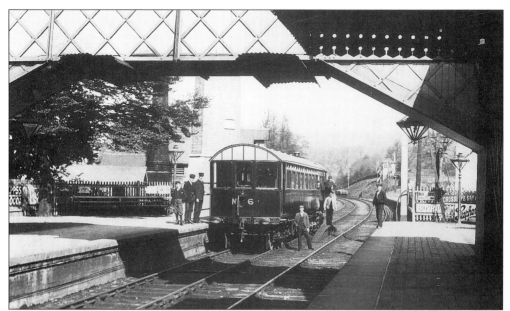

RAILCAR, STROUD G.W.R. STATION. When this fine photograph was taken, c. 1905, the railcars which served the Stroud valleys were still something of a novelty. Here Lee has persuaded several station staff and bystanders to pose for him. Note the advertising plaques, the brewery chimney and the signal box in the background. (Compare this with the view of Stroud G.W.R. station on page 75 and a further railcar photograph on page 24.)

G.W.R. MOTOR BUS. On 9 January 1905 the Great Western Railway inaugurated a motor bus service from Stroud to Painswick. This photograph, which dates from soon afterwards, is one of a pair taken from opposite sides of the bus, several of which were brought up from Cornwall, having been commissioned initially to serve the Lizard Peninsula.

PIPE LAYING, LONDON ROAD, STROUD. In Edwardian days the citizens of Stroud clearly took considerable interest in the civil engineering projects of their day. Advertising boards in the distance promote Rufus Weston, tailor, and the drapery business of Lewis and Godfrey. The near half of the building on the right was demolished when Cornhill was cut through.

A SUCCESSFUL SPORTSMAN. Who this athlete is I have been unable to discover but, to judge from his trophies, he must have reached a fairly high standard of competence. With carpets carefully draped over the garden path and shed, he stands sockless in a decidedly creased pair of knee-length running shorts. The proof of his excellence is displayed proudly by his side.

THREE-LEGGED CHICKEN. W.F. Lee was fascinated by unusual objects and occurrences, as this photograph from his private collection proves.

STROUD U.D.C. STEAM FIRE ENGINE. This splendid photograph shows the Stroud U.D.C. fire engine, one of two which served the town. It was housed in The Shambles. Its captain in 1910 was Jesse Tanner and it was manned by eleven men. An escape ladder extended to 45 feet. The photograph must predate 1909, when William Tanner, engineer and boiler stoker, seen between the hoses, died. The engine, named the 'Queen', had been bought for £294 in 1899 from the manufacturers Merryweather.

STROUD U.D.C. STEAM FIRE ENGINE. In this rather less clear photograph, the same engine is seen in action either in earnest on a call, or at a practice.

DECORATED ARCH, HIGH STREET, STROUD. In 1907 the County Agricultural Show came to Stroud. Shops were liberally decorated and four impressive arches were erected, in High Street, George Street, Gloucester Street and King Street. This detailed photograph shows the early stages of the decoration of the first of these. Note the cart which has just delivered a consignment of greenery.

RUSSELL STREET, 1907 AGRICULTURAL SHOW. Technically this is one of Lee's finest pictures. Its quality and focus are such that, on the original photograph, 'Stroud Urban District Council' may be read on the rear panel of the cart in the far distance. (See pages 33, 50, 58-60 and 106-7.)

KING STREET PARADE, SHOW DAY 1907. The festivities included a decorated vehicle competition. Here the crowd is seen admiring the entries. Lee took this photograph from an upstairs window in Clark's haberdashery store in George Street.

A DRAPER'S BILL. At the period of the Agricultural Show, Gillman's shop was located on King Street Parade. This fascinating bill mentions, amongst other items, Welsh flannel and Turkish dusters.

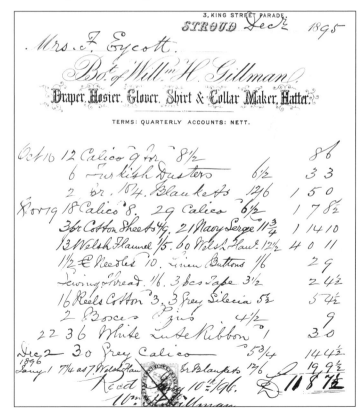

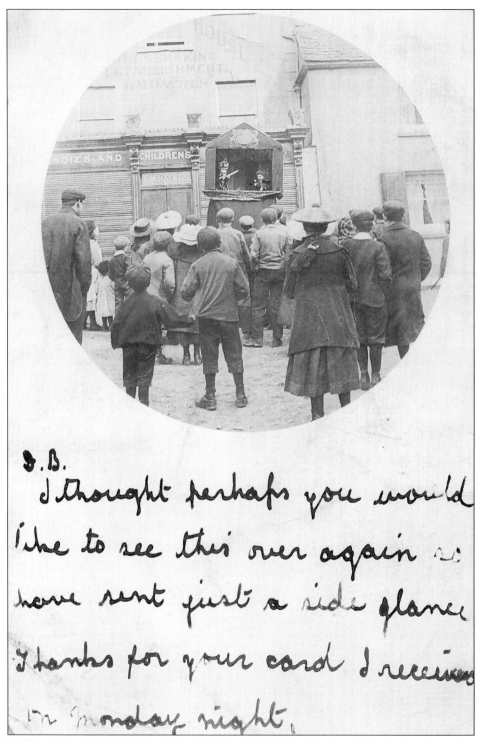

PUNCH AND JUDY SHOW, THE CROSS, STROUD, CIRCA 1904. Perhaps Lee's finest photograph, this atmospheric picture shows the appeal of street entertainment in the days before the advent of television. Note the small boy tugging at his friend's jacket.

Five
William Adams

A gifted amateur photographer, Bill Adams was born at 109, Stratford Road, Stroud. In 1908 he married Gertrude Cooke, daughter of A.S. Cooke the well-known Paganhill builder. The marital home, 'Hazelmere', Coronation Road, Rodborough, was built by his father-in-law.

WILLIAM ADAMS AND HIS WIFE GERTRUDE, c. 1945. This is one of the very few photographs of Bill Adams. It seems that he was happier at the other end of the camera.

A leaning towards chemistry at school kindled Bill's interest in photography and his first camera, a quarter-plate made of cardboard and complete with plates and developer, was bought in a Bristol shop for one shilling. Following the acquisition of more sophisticated equipment, Bill's photograph of Scarborough sea-front was included in a Bristol photographic exhibition in 1906.

Bill Adams was employed as a Post Office supervisor and the local Sub-Post Offices he visited in the course of his work proved to be lucrative outlets for the postcard views he began producing in the 1920s and '30s. Other than harvest scenes taken in the nearby Rodborough fields, these views are mainly limited to Randwick, Painswick and the Chalford valley and can be identified by the distinctive lettering of their captions.

Apart from producing postcards, Bill was in demand as a photographer at weddings and other public functions. He was commissioned by the Stroud Brewery Company to take photographs of some of their licensed houses and also by Anson Dyer Studios during the war years, to supply Aircraft Recognition material for the Civil Defence authorities. He is also remembered as the photographer of the Leonard Stanley ghost! Excavations had revealed the Saxon apse of the Priory Church and, after taking photographs on site, Adams was taken ill. On his recovery he found that the negatives revealed a translucent figure not previously seen, a fact that created much local interest at the time.

Things did not always go to plan and Bill's younger son Geoffrey recalls an occasion at Minchinhampton Market House, when faulty flash powder caused a minor explosion and filled the building with smoke!

Bill Adams was an active and popular member of the local community, a sidesman at Rodborough Church and a former Vice-President of the Old Marlingtonians' Association.

THE BOULEVARDS AND PRINCE ALBERT INN. Surely this must be one of the most attractive parts of Rodborough and compares favourably with many Cotswold village scenes. The name of this inn suggests that it dates from the middle of the nineteenth century.

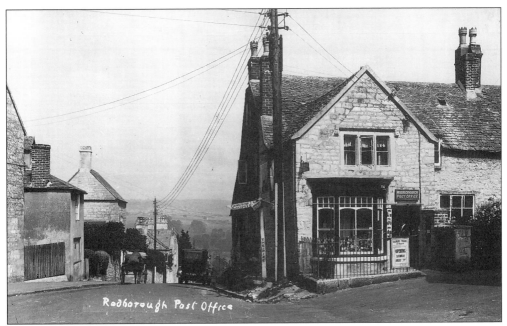

RODBOROUGH POST OFFICE. Quite an agreeable view, despite the web of telephone and electricity wires! The old post office displays a selection of postcards, whilst the placard advertises the opening, which took place in August 1935, of the new Gaumont Cinema in London Road, Stroud, by Jessie Matthews and Sonny Hale.

RODBOROUGH POST OFFICE (DETAIL).

PLOUGHING IN RODBOROUGH FIELDS. The ploughman's skill is demonstrated in this attractive pre-war scene, with Stroud clearly visible between the trees in the background.

MOWING ON THE COTSWOLDS. Another scene in Rodborough fields, but on this occasion the farm worker is accompanied by a young assistant carrying a long hay rake.

HAYMAKING. This attractive view completes the trio, but the postmark date 1924 suggests that it is earlier than its predecessors. All three photographs were taken close to Bill Adams' home, as evidenced by the houses in Coronation Road, visible in the background. This postcard was sent by a visitor 'having a nice time despite unsettled weather' and spending most of his time on the common. (The horse would appear to be the same in all the last three photographs.)

BUTTEROW PIKE, 1933. No doubt this little group was invited to wait while the photograph was taken, possibly in the hope that they would all want copies afterwards! Below the well-known Toll House, which displays its tariff board, a large open tourer stands near Zion Chapel. (Compare this with an earlier photograph of Butterow Pike on page 96.)

BUTTEROW PIKE (DETAIL).

RODBOROUGH HILL. This is one of a number of views taken by Bill Adams, who lived nearby. The card is postmarked 1937 and gives an air of general tidiness. Note that gas lighting is still in use.

SILVER JUBILEE BONFIRE, 1935. The construction of beacons like this one on Rodborough Common would have required considerable expertise and the tradition often passed through the same families for generations. Similar beacons would be built at other vantage points such as Selsley, Painswick and Doverow, involving friendly rivalry between the participants.

RODBOROUGH FORT, 1935. The floodlighting of the fort for King George V's Silver Jubilee provided one of the most spectacular displays in the district. The illuminated 'folly' would have been visible for many miles around. (See also page 98.)

VIEW FROM RODBOROUGH FORT. A panoramic view in which Cainscross Road, Marling School and the early council development at Cashes Green are clearly evident.

TELEPHOTO VIEW OF THE FORT. Apart from the fort, the old gabled cottages at Stanfields and Whitfield's eighteenth-century Tabernacle are included in this telephoto view taken from Selsley.

HOUSE AT STANFIELDS. A closer view of the residence shown in the previous photograph. This fine gabled property dates from 1647 and it is perhaps unfortunate that two of the chimneys have been rebuilt in brick. Note the craftsmanship shown in the stone wall enclosing the field.

THE BEAR HOTEL. This old hostelry was dramatically extended in the 1920s, only the two left-hand gables being original. Rather surprisingly, the two architectural styles have blended well.

VIEW FROM RODBOROUGH COMMON. Much of South Woodchester appears in this photograph which includes Atcombe Terrace on the left and Bospin Lane upper right.

KINGSCOURT AND LITTLE LONDON. Apart from its scenic content, this photograph shows a small section of the old Midland Railway line that ran between Dudbridge and Nailsworth and has since been converted into a cycle track. The bridge, which has been demolished, served the driveway leading to Woodchester Old Priory and the original Woodchester church. The houses in the foreground have also gone.

VIEW FROM SELSLEY HILL. Another panoramic view, this time looking over the rooftops of Stanley Park towards Ebley Mill, Cainscross Church and the early development of Cashes Green. The villages of Randwick and Ruscombe are visible in the distance.

STRATFORD ROAD, STROUD. Adams probably took this photograph shortly after the council house development on the right had been completed by the Stroud Urban District Council in 1929. Little has changed, except that the two youngsters would not be loitering in the middle of this busy road today.

PAGANHILL, STROUD. This view, looking down Stratford Road, is postmarked 1932. The building on the extreme right was demolished many years ago to improve visibility at this busy road junction. Blanch's bakery and shop, on the left, were removed in the 1970s to improve access to a former filling station and car sales area.

THE MAYPOLE, PAGANHILL, 1932. The Maypole is pictured on its site at the junction of the Whiteshill and Ruscombe roads. The grass triangle on which it stood has been much reduced in size, as has the stunted pole which still marks the spot. It is believed that earlier maypoles stood in the grounds of Upfield House, and an unpainted specimen can currently be found in the Old Crown Inn car park. Maypoles could be as much as a hundred feet in height and would last for over twenty years.

PUCKS HOLE, NEAR STROUD. This hamlet, near Paganhill, once possessed a mill, but only the mill house and part of the row of mill cottages remain, both now converted into desirable residences. The cottage gardens in the foreground appear well-tended and the rather motley collection of sheds on the left suggests further horticultural activity.

CAINSCROSS HOSPITAL CARNIVAL, 1923. Many fund-raising events were staged to benefit local hospitals. Adams obviously took a series of photographs (this is number 4) to commemorate the occasion. It looks as though the entire local population turned out to watch!

On the Canal
Near Cainscross

THE CANAL NEAR CAINSCROSS. This is a very different Cainscross scene. The bridge shown carried the main road between Cainscross and Dudbridge. The lock beyond was the last to be negotiated by the motor barge *Kathleen*, which was still collecting crude tar from the Stroud gasworks in the early 1940s.

WHITESHILL FROM THE CHURCH TOWER. Picture postcards of Whiteshill are pretty thin on the ground. This view, one of several taken from the church tower, shows most of the older part of the village, with the Star Inn in the foreground.

RUSCOMBE. In this view, which shows the extent of quarrying in the village, the earlier Zion Hill Chapel can be seen. Stone from this building was used in the twenties to construct the Sunday School adjoining the present chapel, which stands off to the right of the picture.

BULLS CROSS, NEAR SLAD. Rubble has been piled on both sides of the road. (Surely there were no New Age Travellers in the 1920s!) Prospect House dominates the scene and the photograph appears to accentuate the right-hand bend of the road leading to Birdlip. Note the old milestone.

THE THRUPP. From the humpbacked canal bridge, the track leads past the old Phoenix Iron Works towards the main London Road, with the Thrupp terraces beyond. This postcard was sent in 1926 by Miss Edith Waller of Phoenix House; she was clearly a close relative of George Waller, the factory owner.

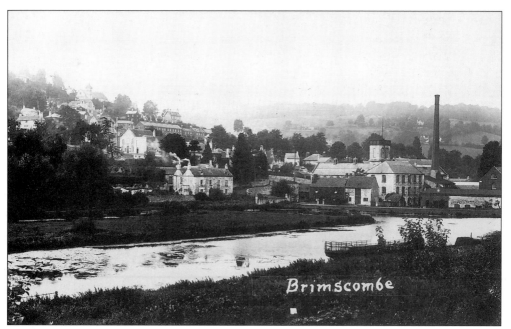

BRIMSCOMBE PORT. Once the proud headquarters of the Thames and Severn Canal Company, Brimscombe Port here shows signs of the dereliction which led to its abandonment in the early 1930s.

LONDON ROAD, BRIMSCOMBE. The numbered caption indicates that Adams took many views of Brimscombe. The large building in the centre was once a mill. Beyond it is the former Port Inn, a hostelry popular with the local bargees. The road has now been straightened and the premises on the right have been demolished.

THE CHALFORD DONKEY. For many years this patient beast and its ancestors proved invaluable in supplying the cottage terraces of Chalford with the necessities of life. Almost every local photographer took similar views and this c. 1930 photograph is believed to show Frank Gardiner, the local baker's boy.

FROGMARSH, WOODCHESTER. Frogmarsh Mill, in the foreground, has had a variety of uses, and for many years was occupied by the Carr Tanning Company. The small ornamental structure on the right, immediately in front of the chimneystack, was removed many years ago and re-erected as a garden pavilion at Bodnant in North Wales.

HIGH STREET, SOUTH WOODCHESTER. This is an excellent example of how human and vehicular activity add interest to a photograph. This c. 1930 scene shows one of the oldest and most interesting parts of the village. The small delivery van outside the post office belonged to Edmonds and Humpidge, seedsmen and florists of George Street, Stroud.